Who Said This?

Write the numeral in the box that explains the sentence.

1. Happy Birthday!
2. I'm high in the sky.
3. I'm so sleepy.
4. This tastes good.
5. I love to read.
6. We won!
7. I like the rain.
8. Did you brush your teeth?

Name _____

Number each row of boxes in 1, 2, 3 order.

Mark Mouse

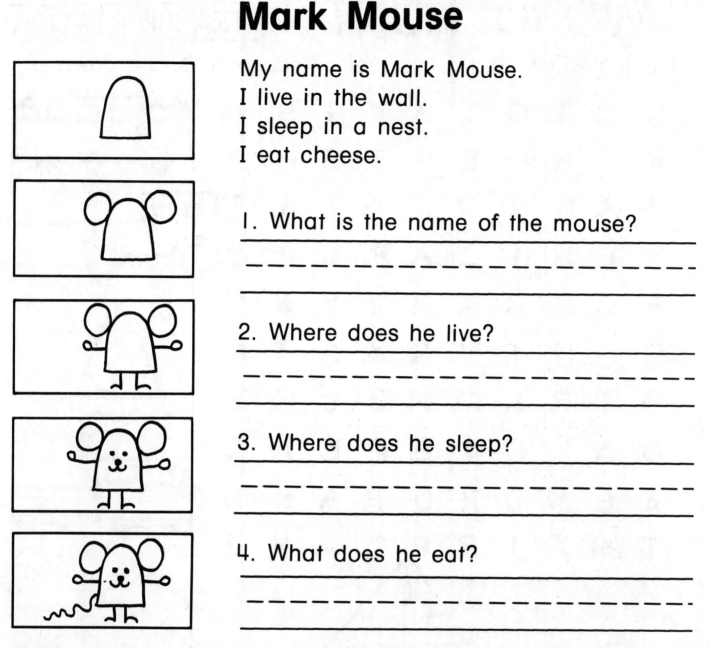

My name is Mark Mouse.
I live in the wall.
I sleep in a nest.
I eat cheese.

1. What is the name of the mouse?

_____

_____

2. Where does he live?

_____

_____

3. Where does he sleep?

_____

_____

4. What does he eat?

_____

_____

Draw Mark Mouse and three friends. Give them some cheese to eat.

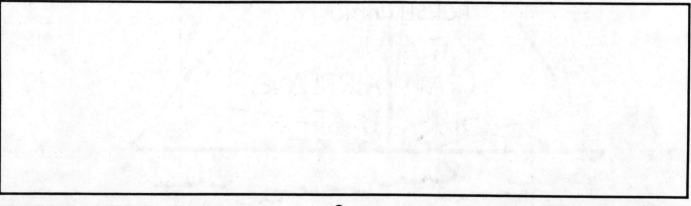

WORD HUNT   TRANSPORTATION

Find the words and circle them. Read across and down.

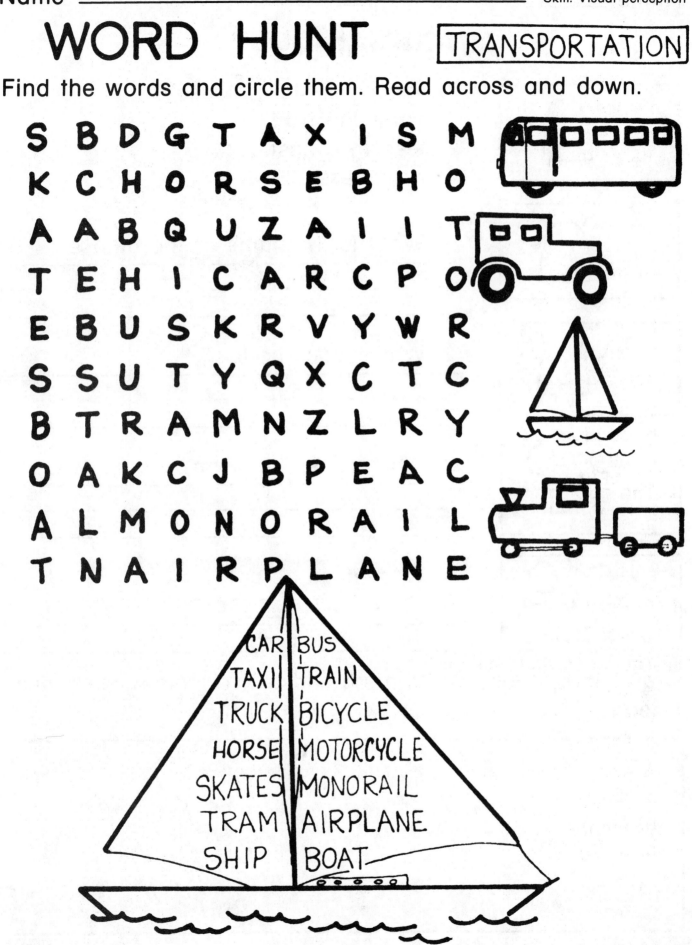

```
S B D G T A X I S M
K C H O R S E B H O
A A B Q U Z A I I T
T E H I C A R C P O
E B U S K R V Y W R
S S U T Y Q X C T C
B T R A M N Z L R Y
O A K C J B P E A C
A L M O N O R A I L
T N A I R P L A N E
```

CAR   BUS
TAXI   TRAIN
TRUCK   BICYCLE
HORSE   MOTORCYCLE
SKATES   MONORAIL
TRAM   AIRPLANE
SHIP   BOAT

Foot Warmer

Put on your shoes! <u>They</u> keep your feet warm and safe. Long **ago**, **some** shoes were made of grass. Others were made of rubber sap from trees. Later, people found they could use animal skins. Today, shoes are made of different things. They come in all sizes, shapes and colors.

1. **In the story, the word <u>shoes</u> means:**
   a. something we wear on our hands
   b. something we wear on our feet
   c. something we wear on our head

2. **Another word for <u>keep</u> is:**
   a. give
   b. send
   c. hold

3. **The opposite of <u>later</u> is:**
   a. sooner
   b. little
   c. any

4. **A word in the story that sounds like <u>maid</u> is:**
   _____

5. **The word <u>they</u> stands for:**
   a. grass
   b. rocks
   c. shoes

6. **A word in the story that means <u>men</u> and <u>women</u> is:**
   a. shoes
   b. people
   c. trees

Name _____

Paste [sail] to [boat] to make a compound word.
Write the new word on the line.

[sail] [boat]

sailboat _ _ _ _ _ _ _ _

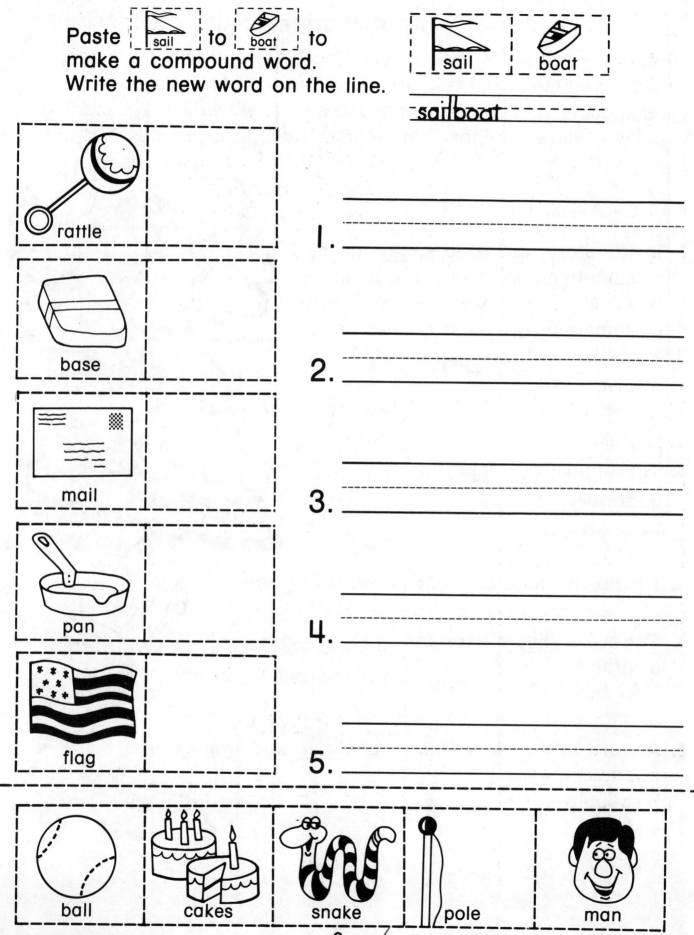

rattle

base

mail

pan

flag

1. _____

2. _____

3. _____

4. _____

5. _____

ball   cakes   snake   pole   man

☐ Draw a yellow straw hat on Mrs. Bear.

☐ Make three red flowers on it.

☐ Do you see the paw that is down? Draw a baby bear by that paw. Baby bear can hold that paw.

☐ Draw a little black dog over by the flower.

☐ Give the dog a little red tongue.

☐ Make a long tail on the dog.

☐ Color the grass brown. It must be very dry.

☐ Make a yellow sun in the sky.

☐ Put a happy face on the sun.

☐ Make a blue bird up in the sky too.

FS-2661 Reading Workbook-Book One

Write the correct word on the line.

1. My _____ is Jane.

2. I am _____ years old.

3. My hair is _____ .

4. My _____ are blue.

ten	name
eyes	black

It is big!

5. We have a big _____ .

6. It has four _____ .

7. Its color is _____ .

8. It can go _____ .

car	fast
red	wheels

Steve's Lizard

Steve's pet is a lizard.

It lives in a cage.

Every day Steve feeds it bugs.

The lizard's name is Lil.

1. Who has a pet?

    _____

    -

2. What is the pet?

    -

3. Where does the pet live?

    _____

    -

4. Who feeds the pet?

    -

5. What does the pet eat?

    -

6. What is the pet's name?

    -

FS-2661 Reading Workbook-Book One

Read the story.

That bird cannot fly. It has a hurt wing. I will take care of it. Then the bird will get well.

Read the sentences below. Cut them out and paste them in the right order.

1	
2	
3	
4	

Cut.

One wing is hurt.

I will help the bird.

The bird will get well.

It cannot fly.

What Tool Would You Use?

Write the numeral under the picture that goes with the sentence.

1. Please cut the bread, John.
2. A nail goes here, Sally.
3. This ice cream tastes yummy.
4. Cut this wood in half, please.
5. Can you hold the bolt tighter?
6. This will help you push the needle, Sue.
7. Cut the paper in half.
8. Mom, the eye is too small.

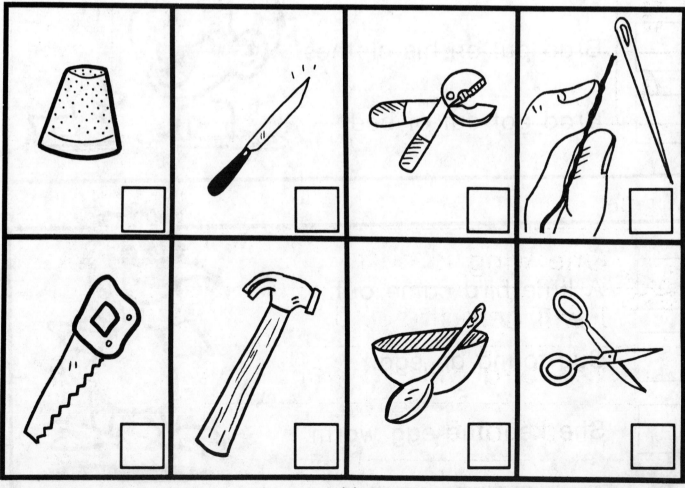

Name _____

Number each row of boxes in 1, 2, 3 order.

1.

☐ She got fruit and milk.

☐ Mona went to the store.

☐ Mona took the food home.

2.

☐ Brad took a bath.

☐ Brad put on his clothes.

☐ Brad got out of bed.

3.

☐ A little bird came out.

☐ Sue found an egg.

☐ She kept the egg warm.

12

The Butterfly

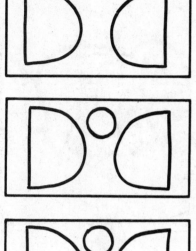

See the red and blue butterfly.
She has spots on her wings.
She lives in a tree.
She flies in the sky.

1. What color is the butterfly?

_ _ _ _ _ _ _ _ _ _ _ _ _ _ _ _ _ _

2. What are on the butterfly's wings?

_ _ _ _ _ _ _ _ _ _ _ _ _ _ _ _ _ _

3. Where does she live?

_ _ _ _ _ _ _ _ _ _ _ _ _ _ _ _ _ _

4. Where does she fly?

_ _ _ _ _ _ _ _ _ _ _ _ _ _ _ _ _ _

Draw some butterflies in the sky.

WORD HUNT FARM ANIMALS

Find the words and circle them. Read across and down.

B T F A R M G C D C
T R A C T O R O M H
A E R Z P L O W R I
L E M B F R I S B C
M S E L D B C R A K
D C R O O S T E R E
A L P I G S K A N N
V E G E T A B L E S
E M Y R H O R S E S
F A R M H O U S E Z

FARM BARN
HORSES TRACTOR
CHICKENS ROOSTER
PIGS FARMER VEGETABLES
DOG TREES FARMHOUSE
PLOW COWS

April Fool!

Can you be sly and fool your friend on April first? You can shout, "Watch out! There is something climbing on your back!" If <u>he</u> becomes frightened, you will yell, "April Fool!" If you lived in France you would say, "April Fish."

1. In the story, the word <u>frightened</u> means:
   a. scared
   b. happy
   c. sad

2. Another word for <u>sly</u> is:
   a. silly
   b. strong
   c. tricky

3. The opposite of <u>on</u> is:
   a. over
   b. off
   c. under

4. In the story, a word that sounds like <u>you're</u> is:

   _____

5. The word <u>he</u> stands for:
   a. your friend
   b. April First
   c. France

6. A word in the story that goes with <u>second</u> and <u>third</u> is:
   a. April
   b. back
   c. first

Name _____

Make a compound word from the two words in each box.
Write the new word on the line.

1. flag + pole

_____

2. base + ball

_____

3. dog + house

_____

4. hair + brush

_____

5. bare + foot

_____

6. play + pen

_____

7. butter + fly

_____

8. lady + bug

_____

9. shoe + lace

_____

10. cup + cake

_____

Fred wants to catch the ball.
- ☐ Draw a glove on the hand that is up.
- ☐ Color Fred's cap orange.
- ☐ Draw some green grass for him to stand on.
- ☐ Make a ball in the top right corner.
- ☐ Color Fred's shoes orange.
- ☐ Do you see the number on his shirt? Color it orange. **ange.**
- ☐ Color the rest of his clothes light purple.
- ☐ Make Fred's tongue red.

I think he is going to fall.
- ☐ Draw a little red pillow behind him. That may help.
- ☐ Make a little black dot in the top left corner. Make it tiny.

I don't know why. Do you?

Write the correct word on the line.

1. I _____ my dog.

2. My _____ loves me.

3. He sleeps in my _____ .

4. He loves to eat _____ .

cheese	bed
love	dog

5. One, two, _____ .

6. Four, _____ , six.

7. Seven, eight, nine, _____ .

8. See, I can _____ .

ten	three
five	count

FS-2661   Reading Workbook-Book One

The Sick Cat

Mrs. Brown's cat is sick.

Mrs. Brown went to work.

Jane said she would take care of the cat.

She fed her warm milk.

The cat is better now.

1. Who has a cat?

_____

2. What is wrong with the cat?

_____

3. Where did Mrs. Brown go?

_____

4. What did Jane say she would do?

_____

5. What did Jane feed the cat?

_____

6. How does the cat feel now?

_____

Read the story.

Mike looked at his bike. "Oh no, I have a flat tire," he said. "I will fix it now. Then I will pump up the tire."

Read the sentences below. Cut them out and paste them in the right order.

1	
2	
3	
4	

Cut.

He will fix it.

Mike saw the flat tire.

Mike will pump air in the tire.

"Oh no, I have a flat tire."

All About Christmas!

Write the numeral in the box that explains the sentence.

1. He had a very shiny nose.
2. He brings presents.
3. The Christmas balls keep falling off.
4. No two are ever alike.
5. We need coal, a carrot and a hat.
6. Hang it on the chimney.

Number each row of boxes in 1, 2, 3 order.

1.
☐ Then he got one tooth.

☐ Now he has ten teeth!

☐ Joe was a tiny baby.

2.
☐ Her dog had two puppies.

☐ Pam had one dog.

☐ Now Pam has three dogs.

3.
☐ He ate it all up.

☐ Dad made some toast.

☐ He put jam on it.

Name _____

Wanda the Whale

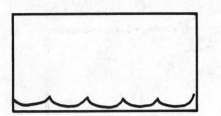

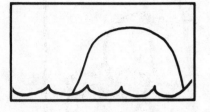

Wanda is a whale.
She has a big tail.
Air comes out of her blow-hole.
She swims many miles.

1. What is Wanda?

_ _ _ _ _ _ _ _ _ _ _ _ _ _ _ _ _ _ _

2. Is her tail big or small?

_ _ _ _ _ _ _ _ _ _ _ _ _ _ _ _ _ _ _

3. What comes out of her blow-hole?

_ _ _ _ _ _ _ _ _ _ _ _ _ _ _ _ _ _ _

4. How far does Wanda swim?

_ _ _ _ _ _ _ _ _ _ _ _ _ _ _ _ _ _ _

Draw Wanda. Make her swimming in blue water.

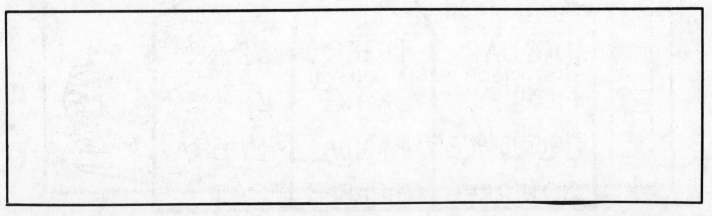

WORD HUNT   ZOO ANIMALS

Find the words and circle them. Read across and down.

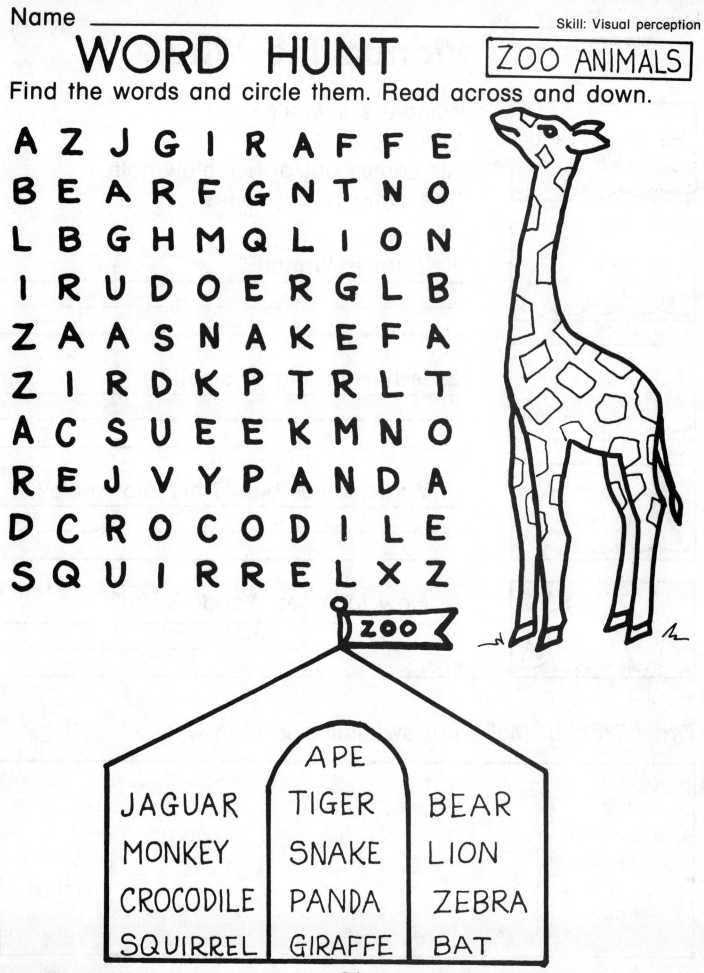

```
A Z J G I R A F F E
B E A R F G N T N O
L B G H M Q L I O N
I R U D O E R G L B
Z A A S N A K E F A
Z I R D K P T R L T
A C S U E E K M N O
R E J V Y P A N D A
D C R O C O D I L E
S Q U I R R E L X Z
```

ZOO

JAGUAR	APE	BEAR
	TIGER	
MONKEY	SNAKE	LION
CROCODILE	PANDA	ZEBRA
SQUIRREL	GIRAFFE	BAT

    24   FS-2661 Reading Workbook-Book One

Paddle Your Own Canoe

Have you ever been in a canoe? You must be careful when you get in. If you do not bend low <u>it</u> might tip. Be sure to sit while you are moving. Then you will have a smooth trip.

1. In the story, the word <u>canoe</u> means:
   a. a kind of candy
   b. a kind of boat
   c. a kind of animal

2. Another word for <u>must</u> is:
   a. should
   b. won't
   c. find

3. The opposite of <u>low</u> is:
   a. angry
   b. happy
   c. high

4. A word in the story that sounds like <u>bin</u> is:

   _____

5. The word <u>it</u> stands for:
   a. the canoe
   b. you
   c. me

6. A word in the story that goes with <u>sailboat</u> and <u>rowboat</u> is:
   a. careful
   b. canoe
   c. knees

Write the two words that make up each compound word.

1. blueberry
_____
_____

2. popcorn
_____
_____

3. football
_____
_____

4. downstairs
_____
_____

5. sidewalk
_____
_____

6. raincoat
_____
_____

7. outside
_____
_____

8. beehive
_____
_____

9. snowstorm
_____
_____

10. cowboy
_____
_____

☐ Mom has a rattle for the baby. Draw it in her hand.

☐ Dad has an apple for the baby. Draw it in his hand.

☐ Color Mom's dress green and yellow.

☐ Make her shoes brown.

☐ Color Dad's pants dark blue.

☐ Make his shirt light blue.

☐ Color his shoes black.

☐ Make a little yellow rug under the baby.

☐ Draw a little red ball on the floor.

☐ Draw a little toy bear on the floor too.

Name _____

Write the correct word on the line.

I know that . . .

1. I can _____ a book.

2. I can _____ a cookie.

3. I can _____ a bike.

4. I can _____ a kite.

fly	read
eat	ride

5. A _____ is in the water.

6. A _____ is in the sky.

7. A _____ is in the tree.

8. A boy can _____ .

boat	jet
skate	cat

Twins

Joe and Pam are twins.

They swim in the lake.

They play ball in the park.

At night they do their homework.

After school they skate on twin skateboards.

1. What is the name of Joe's sister?

_____

2. What is the name of Pam's brother?

_____

3. Where do they swim?

_____

4. Where do they play ball?

_____

5. What do they do at night?

_____

6. What do they do after school?

_____

Read the story.

Nan hears a bell. She runs to get her money. Now she sees the red truck. She wants to buy ice cream.

Read the sentences below. Cut them out and paste them in the right order.

1	
2	
3	
4	

Cut.

Nan gets her money.

She can see the red truck.

The bell is ringing.

Nan will buy ice cream.

What's the Weather?

Write the numeral in the box that explains the sentence.

1. Now we can ski.
2. Teddy needs an umbrella today.
3. It was hard to see across the street.
4. My kite flew as high as I could see.
5. We are ready for the beach.
6. I think it will rain today.

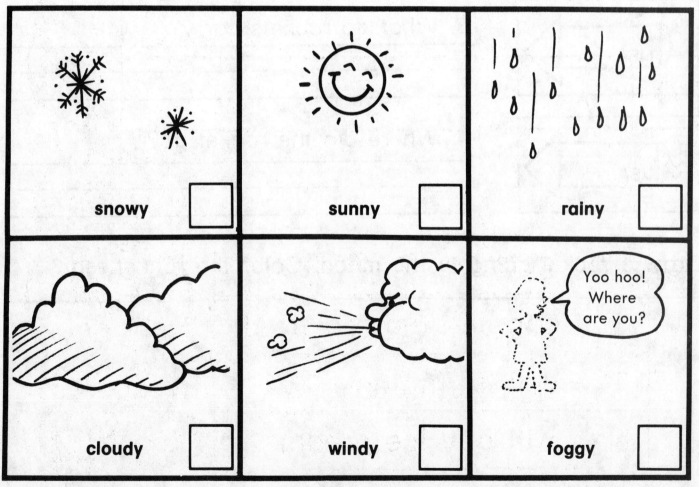

snowy ☐   sunny ☐   rainy ☐

cloudy ☐   windy ☐   foggy ☐

Yoo hoo! Where are you?

31

Rockets

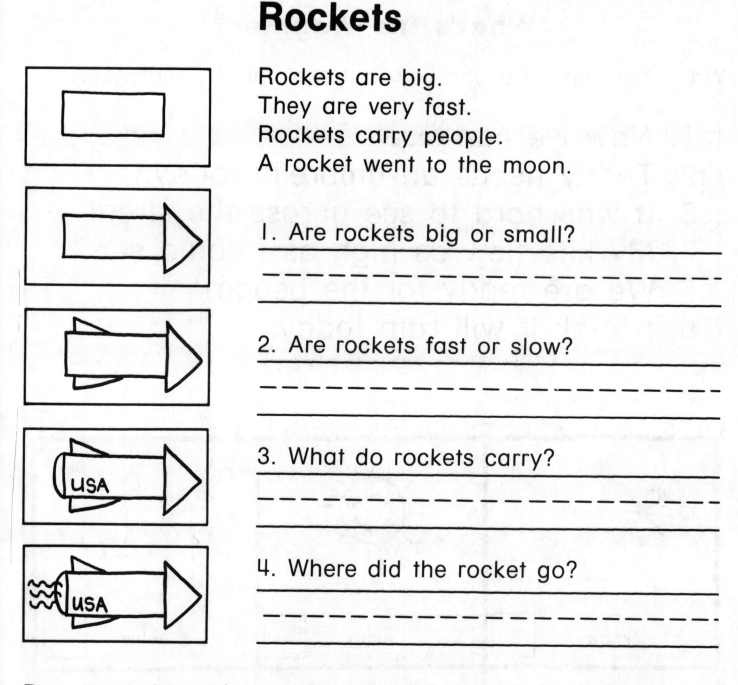

Rockets are big.
They are very fast.
Rockets carry people.
A rocket went to the moon.

1. Are rockets big or small?

   -

2. Are rockets fast or slow?

   -

3. What do rockets carry?

   -

4. Where did the rocket go?

   -

Draw a rocket going to the moon. Color the rocket red.

WORD HUNT

INSTRUMENTS

Find the words and circle them. Read across and down.

```
C L A R I N E T B D
K F V I O L A R J U
M P I A N O I U E K
P G O O D R U M G U
V G L R Q B D P F L
F U I G X A U E L E
O I N A B S R T U L
M T K N P S Z H T E
S A X O P H O N E I
W R L N Y C S E J T
```

VIOLIN   PIANO   TRUMPET

FLUTE   DRUM   SAXOPHONE

ORGAN   VIOLA   GUITAR

UKULELE   BASS   CLARINET

The Apple Man

Johnny Appleseed traveled west when our country was new. His real name was John Chapman. He planted many apple seeds in Ohio and Indiana. He cared for the young trees. At first people called him "the apple seed man." Then they called him "Johnny Appleseed."

1. **In the story, the word <u>traveled</u> means:**
   a. stayed home
   b. spoke softly
   c. went from one place to another

2. **Another word for <u>real</u> is:**
   a. true
   b. fake
   c. long

3. **The opposite of <u>west</u> is:**
   a. first
   b. east
   c. last

4. **A word in the story that sounds like <u>four</u> is:**
   _____

5. **The word <u>he</u> stands for:**
   a. Johnny Appleseed
   b. apples
   c. trees

6. **A word in the story that goes with <u>peaches</u> and <u>pears</u> is:**
   a. people
   b. apples
   c. west

SEEDS

Write the missing compound word in each sentence.

| sunshine | anyone | fireman | myself | baseball |
| pancakes | birthday | afternoon | doorbell | airplane |

1. Dad is a _____.

2. I ate two _____.

3. Is _____ home?

4. Let's play _____.

5. I saw Kim this _____.

6. The _____ is bright.

7. Today is my _____.

8. I walked home by _____.

9. Let's fly in the _____.

10. Ring the _____.

35

Kelly likes to show off.

☐ Color her shorts green.

☐ Put red and white stripes on her shirt.

☐ Color her hair bright orange.

☐ Color the band in her hair green.

☐ Make her skateboard purple.

☐ Draw six little hairs on her legs.

☐ Make a black and blue spot on her knee.

☐ Put a red spot on one elbow.

☐ Draw a banana peel on the walk in front of her.

☐ Draw a doctor with a black bag behind her.

Look out, Kelly!

FS-2661   Reading Workbook-Book One

Write the correct word on the line.

1. Apples are _____ .

2. The _____ is green.

3. A pumpkin is _____ .

4. The _____ is blue.

yummy

| sky   grass |
| red   orange |

5. You can run _____ .

6. I can climb a _____ .

7. We can _____ hands.

8. My pet _____ can fly.

| fast   bird |
| tree   shake |

Read the story.

Watch me mix a new color! First I will put some white paint in the dish. Now I will add red paint. I made pink paint.

Read the sentences below. Cut them out and paste them in the right order.

1	
2	
3	
4	

Cut.

I will add red paint.

Look at the new color.

I will put white paint in the dish.

Watch me mix a new color!

Saving Stamps

My friend Fred and I save stamps.

We have four books of stamps.

On Saturdays we go to the stamp store.

We look to see what is new.

Sometimes we buy stamps.

1. What is my friend's name?

_____

_____

2. What do we save?

_____

_____

3. How many books of stamps do we have?

_____

_____

4. When do we go to the stamp store?

_____

_____

5. What do we look to see?

_____

_____

6. What do we do sometimes?

_____

_____

Use Your Senses

Write the numeral in the box that explains the sentence.

1. The girl is singing.
2. The skunk is angry.
3. The food is good.
4. The trees are green.
5. The stove is hot.

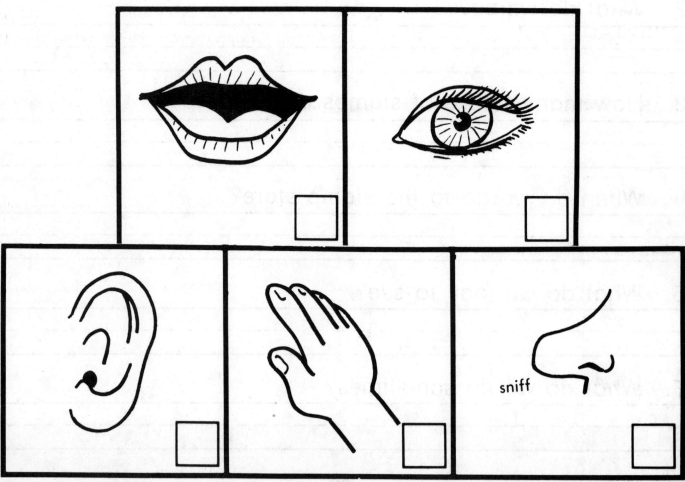

sniff

Henry Hedgehog

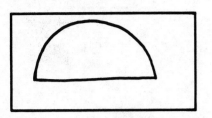

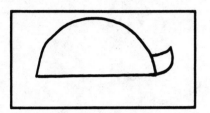

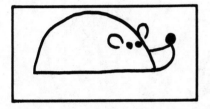

This is Henry Hedgehog.
He has sharp things on his back.
He has a funny nose.
He can roll into a ball.

1. What is the hedgehog's name?

_____

- - - - - - - - - - - - - - - - - -

2. What does he have on his back?

_____

- - - - - - - - - - - - - - - - - -

3. What is funny?

_____

- - - - - - - - - - - - - - - - - -

4. What can he roll into?

_____

- - - - - - - - - - - - - - - - - -

Draw three hedgehogs. Color them brown.

FS-2661 Reading Workbook-Book One

WORD HUNT

GAMES

Find the words and circle them. Read across and down.

```
B H O P S C O T C H
A S C R A B B L E O
T P I N G P O N G R
T E C D I F I S H S
L C H E C K E R S E
E A E C W E R F G S
S R S B C A R D S H
H O S A J K H K M O
I M O N O P O L Y E
P S D O M I N O E S
```

CHESS		CARDS
SCRABBLE	CHECKERS	HORSESHOES	HOPSCOTCH
MONOPOLY	PING PONG	BATTLESHIP	DOMINOES
		CAROMS	FISH

About Deer

Deer are beautiful animals. They run swiftly and <u>they</u> can jump high. There are many different kinds of deer. One of the strangest is the "barking deer" of China. It barks like a dog when <u>it</u> is frightened. Most of the time <u>it</u> hides in tall grass.

1. In the story, the word <u>swiftly</u> means:
   a. slowly
   b. quickly
   c. dull

2. Another word for <u>beautiful</u> is:
   a. pretty
   b. blue
   c. funny

3. The opposite of <u>tall</u> is:
   a. short
   b. green
   c. also

4. A word in the story that sounds like <u>dear</u> is:

   _____

5. The word <u>they</u> stands for:
   a. China
   b. deer
   c. grass

6. A word in the story that goes with <u>meowing</u> and <u>mooing</u> is:
   a. barking
   b. beautiful
   c. strangest

Find a word in the box to go with each meaning.
Write the compound word on the line.

bookcase	driveway	shoelace	cupboard	doorbell
bathtub	mailbox	bedroom	classroom	doorknob

1. a place for letters _____

2. a place to sleep _____

3. for tying shoes _____

4. a place for books _____

5. for taking a bath _____

6. a place to learn _____

7. use to open door _____

8. place for dishes _____

9. place for the car _____

10. tells you someone is at the door _____

Here comes the school bus!

☐ Write **SCHOOL** on the side of the bus. Spell it right!

☐ Color the bus yellow.

☐ Do you see the boy with the cap? Draw an ear on him.

☐ Color his cap red and give him a little bit of black hair.

☐ Do you see the little girl? Put a green bow on top of her hair.

☐ Draw a girl with brown hair in the back seat.

☐ Draw a man up front. He will drive the bus.

☐ Make a blue cap on his head.

☐ Draw a black road under the tires.

☐ Leave the tires white.

Toot toot!

Name _____

Write the correct word on the line.

1. One and one are _____ .

2. Two and two are _____ .

3. I can _____ .

4. Can _____ ?

add	you
two	four

5. Happy _____ to you.

6. _____ birthday to you.

7. Happy birthday dear _____ .

8. Happy birthday to _____ .

you	Happy
Billy	birthday

Answers

Page One
3., 1., 2., 7.
4., 6., 5., 8.

Page Two
1. 3, 2, 1
2. 2, 1, 3
3. 3, 1, 2
4. 1, 2, 3

Page Three
1. Mark
2. in the wall
3. in a nest
4. cheese

Page Four

Page Five
1. b. something we wear on our feet
2. c. hold
3. a. sooner
4. made
5. c. shoes
6. b. people

Page Six
1. rattlesnake
2. baseball
3. mailman
4. pancakes
5. flagpole

Page Eight
1. name
2. ten
3. black
4. eyes
5. car
6. wheels
7. red
8. fast

Page Nine
1. Steve
2. a lizard
3. in a cage
4. Steve
5. bugs
6. Lil

Page Ten
1. It cannot fly.
2. One wing is hurt.
3. I will help the bird.
4. The bird will get well.

Page Eleven
6., 1., 5., 8.
4., 2., 3., 7.

Page Twelve
1. 2	2. 2	3. 3
1	3	1
3	1	2

Page Thirteen
1. red and blue
2. spots
3. in a tree
4. in the sky

Page Fourteen

Page Fifteen
1. a. scared
2. c. tricky
3. b. off
4. your
5. a. your friend
6. c. first

Page Sixteen
1. flagpole
2. baseball
3. doghouse
4. hairbrush
5. barefoot
6. playpen
7. butterfly
8. ladybug
9. shoelace
10. cupcake

Page Eighteen
1. love
2. dog
3. bed
4. cheese
5. three
6. five
7. ten
8. count

Page Nineteen
1. Mrs. Brown
2. The cat is sick.
3. to work
4. take care of the cat
5. warm milk
6. better

Page Twenty
1. Mike saw the flat tire.
2. "Oh no, I have a flat tire."
3. He will fix it.
4. Mike will pump air in the tire.

Page Twenty-One
3., 6., 1.
2., 4., 5.

Page Twenty-Two
1. 2	2. 2	3. 3
3	1	1
1	3	2

Page Twenty-Three
1. a whale
2. big
3. air
4. many miles

Page Twenty-Four

Page Twenty-Five
1. b. a kind of boat
2. a. should
3. c. high
4. been
5. a. the canoe
6. b. canoe

Page Twenty-Six
1. blue, berry
2. pop, corn
3. foot, ball
4. down, stairs
5. side, walk
6. rain, coat
7. out, side
8. bee, hive
9. snow, storm
10. cow, boy

Page Twenty-Eight
1. read
2. eat
3. ride
4. fly
5. boat
6. jet
7. cat
8. skate

FS-2661 Reading Workbook-Book One

Answers

Page Twenty-Nine
1. Pam
2. Joe
3. in the lake
4. in the park
5. their homework
6. skate on twin skateboards

Page Thirty
1. The bell is ringing.
2. Nan gets her money.
3. She can see the red truck.
4. Nan will buy ice cream.

Page Thirty-One
1., 5., 2.
6., 4., 3.

Page Thirty-Two
1. big
2. fast
3. people
4. to the moon

Page Thirty-Three

Page Thirty-Four
1. c. went from one place to another
2. a. true
3. b. east
4. for
5. a. Johnny Appleseed
6. b. apples

Page Thirty-Five
1. fireman
2. pancakes
3. anyone
4. baseball
5. afternoon
6. sunshine
7. birthday
8. myself
9. airplane
10. doorbell

Page Thirty-Seven
1. red
2. grass
3. orange
4. sky
5. fast
6. tree
7. shake
8. bird

Page Thirty-Eight
1. Watch me mix a new color!
2. I will put white paint in the dish.
3. I will add red paint.
4. Look at the new color.

Page Thirty-Nine
1. Fred
2. stamps
3. four
4. on Saturdays
5. what is new
6. buy stamps

Page Forty
3., 4.
1., 5., 2.

Page Forty-One
1. Henry
2. sharp things
3. his nose
4. a ball

Page Forty-Two

Page Forty-Three
1. b. quickly
2. a. pretty
3. a. short
4. deer
5. b. deer
6. a. barking

Page Forty-Four
1. mailbox
2. bedroom
3. shoelace
4. bookcase
5. bathtub
6. classroom
7. doorknob
8. cupboard
9. driveway
10. doorbell

Page Forty-Six
1. two
2. four
3. add
4. you
5. birthday
6. Happy
7. Billy
8. you